BOOKS ON HORSEBACK

The Packhorse Librarians of Kentucky

written by
Candice Ransom

illustrated by
Massimiliano Di Lauro

The morning sun has yet to step over the ridge, but the Book Lady is ready. Her real name is Marjorie, but everyone calls her the Book Lady.

She opens the door and clouds drift into her kitchen. Fog or no, she can't be late.

In the warm, sweet barn, she saddles Boots, packs fifty books in two strapped bags, adds napkin-wrapped cornbread—her lunch.

"It's Tuesday, Boots. Thousandsticks route," she says, settling on his back. "People are waiting." She nudges the horse into the mist.

It is 1936, and times are hard in America. The Great Depression closed Kentucky's coal mines, putting men out of work. Isolated families have no electricity, telephones, or radios. They need books to learn about the outside world, to get better jobs, to pass the long, dark nights.

Most people live far from public libraries, and few roads carve the hollows and coves.

But with President Franklin Roosevelt's special program, libraries will go to the people.

Women on horseback, carrying donated books.

Now Boots treads a dry creek bed cut through rocky hills. Marjorie talks to fill the miles.

"Empty hands, all wanting books. More hands than books. Still, we do what we can, don't we, Boots?"

In answer, Boots' left ear points to three November crows. His right ear flicks at a quick-footed fox. Boots isn't Marjorie's horse. She leases him from a farmer. Rider and horse aren't yet sure of each other.

Up sounds a shout. “Book Lady’s a’comin’!”

Eager children and their teacher wait outside Piney Grove School. Hands loop Boots’ reins over the rail, stroke his nose.

“Book Lady! What did you bring us?”

She unstraps a saddle bag, lifts a twine-tied stack.

“Geography, history, arithmetic,” the teacher lists. “And storybooks!”

“Not enough for thirty hungry minds. Maybe I’ll have more next trip.”

Up stony slopes. Down steep ravines to the next stop. At the hamlet of Thousandsticks, young and old wait for books. Hands reach for Boots' bridle. Hands unbuckle heavy leather bags.

Marjorie dismounts to distribute books and magazines. "*Treasure Island*, just for you. For you, *Woman's Home Companion*. And here's *Up Creek, Down Creek* for you."

No one notices the books are shabby. No one complains about tattered magazines. They are glad for anything to read, glad for cast-off books from cities like Cincinnati, Pittsburgh, and New York.

All afternoon, Marjorie delivers books to creekside cabins and clapboard churches hard by ivy-cloaked graveyards.

Lonesome people crave conversation as much as magazines and books. Marjorie shares a rice pudding recipe, announces the birth of a new baby, sends healing wishes to the sick.

An old woman gives her a handmade honeysuckle vine basket. “Tote your noon dinner in this.”

Shadows draw over wooded peaks. The horse follows deer traces.

"Last stop," Marjorie tells Boots. "Possum Bend."

Boots droops his head. Elkhorn Creek is deep this time of year. He wades through water up to his hocks.

On the other side, tucked in a pocket hollow, lives a boy too young to read and a mother too far from neighbors. Both are waiting for books.

Marjorie whistles to let them know she's nearby. Down the hill mother and son fly, hand in hand.

"Book Lady, did you bring me a dog story?" the boy asks, same as always.

"Not this time, Charlie. Will *Shoes for Sandy* do instead? I'll read you a little bit."

The boy listens, but Marjorie knows his ears yearn to hear a dog story. President Roosevelt's program pays her wages, but there's no funds for new books. Not even one story for a dog-loving boy.

It's dusky-dark when Boots plods home to his hay barn. Marjorie removes his saddle, grooms his coat, feeds him oats. In her house, she fixes supper.

Tomorrow she and Boots will take a different route. Two weeks will pass until she rides to Possum Bend again. Will she find a dog book in the donation box before then?

She lights a kerosene lamp, flips through newspapers and magazines too torn to circulate. One has photographs of dogs! She will *make* Charlie a dog book!

Her scissors snip pictures of beagle puppies and racing collies, her brush dips into the glue pot. Stout stitching binds the pages.

Outside, buttermilk clouds hide the moon. A sign of falling weather. Cold and sleet are coming. But a homemade dog book waits for a certain boy.

Next morning, icy rain taps windowpanes. Marjorie covers books in protective oilcloth. Then she and Boots set out. Down sleet-slick trails. Between tight-squeeze gaps. Across rushing streams. Will anyone be waiting?

Yes. They stand at slippery footbridges. Under dripping arbors. Beneath tarp-topped lean-tos.

All happy to see the Book Lady.

Afternoon drains into early evening. Soggy vultures sulk on rocky ledges.

"Possum Bend," she says to Boots. "Miles out of our way, but we can do it."

Can they? Boots is tired. One stumble could mean serious trouble for them both.

Run-off sweeps swirls of mud and tree limbs. Boots picks a careful path. Twice, she slides off to guide him.

At last, Elkhorn Creek. Water gushes over its banks.

"Cross here?" she asks Boots.

His ears flatten. No. The horse knows best. She lets him lead.

Boots walks downstream, tests the depth, then plunges in. Water rises to her stirrups but no higher. He straggles up the far-side bank.

The cabin door flings open. "Book Lady!" Charlie cries.

"You're not due for two weeks," his mother says. "Come in out of this sleet!"

Marjorie hands Charlie her handmade book. "Just for you. You don't have to return it in two weeks. It's yours for keeps."

“It’s got dog pictures! I can make up the story!”

And he does, while the Book Lady dries her toes by the fire. Until it’s time to leave.

"Home, Boots." She pats his neck.

Wet and weary, Boots aims for his hay barn at a keen pace.

In the morning, she'll load saddlebags, place her lunch in the honeysuckle basket, turn her horse toward Bear Branch. They are a team.

Gray skies part to let in a slice of starlight. The mountains fall open like the pages of a book, holding them close like hands.

Tomorrow promises to be a fine day.

Readers will be waiting.

Author's Note

This book is based on the true story of packhorse librarians in Kentucky. Marjorie and Boots are fictional characters. It's a story close to my heart because books were (and still are) the most important things to me.

From my childhood home, I could see the purple curves of the Blue Ridge Mountains—the leading edge of the Appalachian Mountain chain—marching like elephants linked tail to trunk. My parents hailed from different parts of the Virginia Appalachians and often talked about the Great Depression. For ten long, weary years, 1929 to 1939, banks closed, few people were employed, and many families struggled to put bread on the table.

The deep, green hills of Eastern Kentucky were hit especially hard. Steep mountains made farming difficult, but men worked in coal mines or sawmills. The Depression shut down mines and logging operations. Without radios, telephones, electricity, or many roads, the people of Appalachia were isolated, forgotten.

Then Franklin D. Roosevelt was elected president in 1933. He vowed to put Americans back to work. He set up federal programs to create new jobs, such as building dams, painting murals in post offices, and developing national parks. One of those projects was the Kentucky Pack Horse Library. Everyone, Roosevelt believed, had the right to read. There were no public libraries in Eastern Kentucky, so libraries would be brought to the people.

The program was simple. Books and other reading materials were carried into the hills by local women on horseback. The mounted librarians earned a monthly salary of $28 (about $500 today). Out of their wages, they leased mules or horses for 50 cents a week and bought the animals' food.

At each county seat, books were catalogued and shelved. Government funds paid the carriers' wages but did not furnish books. Librarians wrote letters to newspapers asking for donations. Soon, boxes of used and discarded books and outdated magazines were shipped to the mountains.

The first packhorse librarians rode out in the fall of 1936—saddlebags, hickory baskets, even pillowcases stuffed with books—to scattered community centers, churches, and schools. Most often, they made deliveries to peoples' homes.

The carriers followed three or four assigned routes a week, averaging eighteen miles a day, 5,000 miles a month. Four packhorse librarians in Leslie County, for example, traveled an area bigger than Delaware to bring books to 8,000 people in a single month.

The women left at dawn and rode in all weather—sleet, snow, pouring rain, blazing heat. The horses and mules played an equally important role. They walked miles every day with loaded packs, following creeks and animal trails over difficult, rugged terrain.

When one librarian's mule died, she walked her eighteen-mile route. When a librarian couldn't cross a rain-swollen river, she spent the night at someone's house. For all their hardships, the packhorse women wished for more books. There were never enough.

Once a week, the carriers met at their county headquarters to mend books. Often, women along their routes would give them a treasured family recipe or quilt pattern. The librarians pasted these recipes and patterns in scrapbooks, which they also circulated. Sometimes they made "picture books" from tattered magazines and newspapers. Bookmarks cut from old Christmas cards were very popular.

The Pack Horse Library Project ended in 1943. America had entered World War II; the Depression was finally over. During the eight years of the program's existence, nearly 1,000 women rode through forty-two Kentucky counties. Countless children learned to read due to the dedication of those women who made hard times a little easier.

Now when I gaze at the Blue Ridge Mountains, I see the misty shapes of horses with their lone riders and faintly hear, "Yonder comes the Book Lady!"

Candice Ransom

is the author of more than 180 books for children and young adults. She lives in Fredericksburg, Virginia, with two impossible cats. Whenever she can, she goes to the nearby Blue Ridge Mountains, part of the Appalachians, with a book and her camera.

Massimiliano Di Lauro

is an Italian illustrator based in Puglia. He has published children's books translated into seven languages, including the award-winning Reycraft Book, *Dolley Madison, the White House, and the Big Tornado*.

A Trip to the BARBERSHOP

written and photographed by
Charles R. Smith Jr.

Dedicated to my grandfather, Richard Bain, who owned a barbershop in Compton, California, and to my dad, Charles R. Smith, who always made his voice heard in the shop.

—C.R.S. Jr.

REYCRAFT SCHOOLHOUSE

Reycraft Schoolhouse
145 Huguenot Street
New Rochelle, NY 10801

reycraftbooks.com

Reycraft Schoolhouse is a line of Reycraft Books, a trade imprint and trademark of Newmark Learning LLC.

Library of Congress Cataloging-in-Publication Data is available.

ISBN: 978-1-4788-9111-6 (A)

Photos: Charles R. Smith Jr.
Author photo: Courtesy of Charles R. Smith Jr.

Printed in Dongguan, China. 949559/0525/22873
10 9 8 7 6 5 4 3 2 1

First Edition published by Reycraft Schoolhouse 2025.

Reycraft Books and Newmark Learning LLC support diversity and the First Amendment, and celebrate the right to read.

BarberKing
OPEN
PULL
BARBER SHOP
WALK-INS WELCOME

"You're looking a little shaggy, Phineas," says Mom. "We need to make a stop before we visit Dad at work."

When Caleb and I need a new haircut, we're off to Barber King, our local barbershop.

As we walk up to the door, I see Santiago and his dad, Ramon. Santiago looks a little shaggy, too!

Ramon and Curtis work as barbers at the shop. Sammy is the owner, and he cuts hair too!

Barber King does a lot for our community, like giving kids backpacks and back-to-school haircuts for free.

Sammy always says,

"When you look good, you feel good."

Buzz buzz buzz
talk talk talk

is all you hear
when you step into the shop.

Talk talk talk
talks the person in the chair.

Talk talk talk

talks the barber cutting hair.

Familiar faces from the neighborhood fill the shop.

Sometimes the talk is about **who's better** or **who's best** in sports teams, music, or movies.

Sometimes people tell stories about where they're from. Sometimes a man gives advice or talks about when he was young. Sometimes a kid tells silly jokes. You can always learn something.

Santiago is Ramon's first customer today.

Ramon **buzz** buzz clips Santiago's hair.

REYCRAFT
WEEKEND AND ZAR SATURDAY SCHOOL

Dameik and I pick books from the little library.

Sometimes it's hard to wait.

But the time goes faster with a fun book.

Now it's finally time for Caleb and me to take a seat in Curtis and Sammy's chairs.

Mom tells the barbers just what to do.

Curtis **combs** combs cuts
Caleb's long hair.

Sammy **buzz buzz snips**
my hair.

Sometimes the clippers can
scare scare scare

when they
buzz buzz buzz
near my ears.

Dameik needs a trim and a fade.
Curtis ties back the braids and gets to work.

Buzz buzz buzz
go the clippers.

The spritz spritz spritz

of the spray begins,

and the dust dust dust

of the brush brings the haircuts to an end.

A spin in the chair
to admire the hair . . .

I look in the mirror and give
a thumbs-up and a smile.
"Thank you!"

Smiles from Curtis, Ramon, and Sammy mean our new cuts look good.

And just like Sammy always says,

"When you look good, you feel good."

Mom gives me money to pay for our haircuts.

Then we say goodbye to all our neighbors and friends.

See you next time at the barbershop, the heart of our community.

Charles R. Smith Jr.

is an award-winning children's book author, photographer, and poet. Born and raised in Southern California, Charles spent many Saturdays with his father in the barbershop. As an adult, Charles decided to cut off all his hair and go bald. Though he enjoys not having to get his hair cut, he misses the discussions and laughter in the barbershop, and he hopes this book captures that same spirit.